CLASS 55
DELTICS

From the Final Years to Preservation

Colin Alexander and Ian Beattie

AMBERLEY

First published 2016

Amberley Publishing
The Hill, Stroud
Gloucestershire, GL5 4EP

www.amberley-books.com

Copyright © Colin Alexander and
Ian Beattie, 2016

The right of Colin Alexander and Ian Beattie
to be identified as the Authors of this work has
been asserted in accordance with the Copyrights,
Designs and Patents Act 1988.

ISBN 978 1 4456 5695 3 (print)
ISBN 978 1 4456 5696 0 (ebook)

British Library Cataloguing in Publication Data.
A catalogue record for this book is available from
the British Library.

Typesetting by Amberley Publishing.
Printed in the UK.

Introduction

The year 2016 marks fifty-five years since the first of the production Deltics, later Class 55, were delivered to the Eastern, North Eastern and Scottish regions of British Railways, where they revolutionised East Coast Main Line services with their unprecedented speeds, levels of utilisation and mileages. They were worthy successors to the Pacifics of Gresley and Peppercorn.

The intention of this publication is to illustrate that brief but fascinating time on BR when the distinguished career of the Deltic fleet was coming to a close. The images are in chronological order as far as possible, and the majority of them date from 1979 onwards. They take us through 1980 to withdrawal at the end of 1981, the Doncaster 'limbo' of 1982 and into the happier days of the preservation era and modern railtours.

My co-contributor Ian Beattie and I first met at Newcastle Central station in 1979 and we have shared a love of Deltics ever since. Ian was lucky enough to own a Pentax K1000 camera at the age of thirteen, and somehow managed to carry it around some dodgy lineside locations without any hassle. I meanwhile made do for a long time with a Kodak Instamatic, which nobody would ever want to steal. This book is a collection of photographs and personal memories from our encounters with the magnificent English Electric/Napier Deltics.

We make no apology for the geographical bias of photographs towards Tyneside, but we have tried to include as many other locations as possible.

When we were in our early teenage years, it was possible to buy a 'Northumbrian Ranger', which, for £2.60, gave unlimited travel for a whole week on the 147 miles of East Coast Main Line between Berwick and York, as well as the lines to Carlisle, Whitby, and so on. In 1980, to celebrate the end of my O Level exams, I treated myself to a First Class Eastern Region Railrover, featuring over 5,000 miles on fourteen different Deltics in a week between Berwick and London!

By this time the InterCity 125 High Speed Train fleet had relegated the Deltics from principal East Coast Main Line services. The Napier machines could be found on the 05.50 King's Cross–Aberdeen (1S12) and its southbound equivalent, 1E26, as well as on the Edinburgh–Plymouth services north of York (1V93 and 1S27), York–London stopping services and Newcastle–Edinburgh 'stoppers'. These were quite different in character, with the York–London trains being composed of Mk2 air-conditioned stock, calling at the likes of Doncaster and Peterborough, while the Edinburgh services were short rakes of steam-heated Mk1s, which stopped at lonely outposts like Chathill with its gas lamps. Chathill probably saw peak passenger numbers in those days, namely us, although we never left the station. If we took 1S15, intending to catch 1E29 back home to Newcastle, there was a minus-one-minute connection at Berwick. Only the brave or insane would risk this. The alternative was to jump off at Chathill and wait on the footbridge. We knew by the distant noise long before the southbound train appeared if it was going to be a Deltic.

As you can imagine, most school holidays and weekends were spent either at Central station or, when we could afford it, travelling up and down the ECML on Deltics, Class 40s and other lesser traction, as well as the occasional jaunt across to Carlisle Citadel and Kingmoor to observe such exotica as classes 26 and 27, and all seven classes of AC electrics then in use.

Before mobile phones and the internet, reliable 'gen' was scarce, but Ian had friends at Benfield and Breckenbeds schools, which boasted lineside views of the ECML at Heaton and Gateshead respectively. They would phone him on the landline and let him know what had been on Plymouth and Carlisle workings so he could decide whether to go to the Central after school or not.

In these General Motors-dominated days, it is easy to forget what variety there was back then, even if it *was* all blue and yellow. Central station had its Class 03 station pilots and, on a typical day, we would see Classes 31, 37, 40, 45, 46, 47 and 55 – but it was our beloved Deltics that most held our attention. We thrilled to the sound of their twin Napier engines and were always disappointed when a 'Duff' or a 'Peak' turned up on a potential Deltic working. Gateshead's fleet of six were invariably filthy, and I always had a soft spot for Finsbury Park's 'racehorses', with their short, quirky names.

As the 1980s began, Nos 55001 *St. Paddy* and 55020 *Nimbus* had already hauled their last trains. Money was short and, once we knew that the Deltics' days on BR were numbered, there was a clamour to buy tickets for as many farewell railtours as possible. The Deltic Preservation Society had established itself by then, and I had volunteered to be the regional coordinator for Tyne & Wear. We could not have dreamed then that, thirty-five years later, the DPS would own three of the six preserved Deltics, and that we could still enjoy the magical Napier sound well into the twenty-first century on main-line railtours.

I would like to dedicate this book to my dad, Jack Alexander MBE, for giving me my lifelong interest in railways, and to all of those hardworking volunteers who have given so much to keep those six surviving Deltics going. Lastly, I must say a massive thank you to Ian Beattie for contributing most of the better-quality pre-digital photographs to this volume.

Colin Alexander

The way it used to be. King's Cross station on 10 August 1962, taken by a sadly departed friend of my dad's, Dave Gordon, who gave the transparency to me. D9003 *Meld* is just over a year old here as she stands alongside BR Standard Britannia Pacific No. 70038 *Robin Hood*. Only about eight years separate the building of the two locomotives, but you wouldn't think it!

In the early 1970s, No. 9019 *Royal Highland Fusilier* crosses the famous diamond crossing as she heads north out of Newcastle Central, viewed from the Norman Castle Keep. North and South Tyneside DMUs stand in platforms 1, 2, 5 & 7. Most of these are now a car park and the diamond crossings are no more. This is one of my dad's slides, and one of my all-time childhood favourites.

No. 9017 *The Durham Light Infantry* near Sessay on the racing stretch in the Vale of York with 1E05, the Up *Flying Scotsman*, circa 1972. Scanned from one of my Dad's negatives. This was a favourite spot to watch the trains go by, accompanied by egg and tomato sandwiches and a flask of tea.

In mid-August 1979, No. 55010 *The King's Own Scottish Borderer* made a rare visit to South Gosforth depot for wheel turning. South Gosforth had been the home of the NER's electric multiple-unit fleet and later BR's DMUs, but locomotives as glamorous as this were seldom seen. Here No. 55010 is in the company of newly delivered Tyne & Wear Metro 'Supertrams', which were to enter service a year later.

Two years before Deltic railtours were to become an almost weekly feature, on 7 October 1979 No. 55022 *Royal Scots Grey* is in charge of the 'Deltic Pioneer' at Newcastle Central's platform 9. This was a circular tour from Manchester Victoria via Carlisle to Newcastle and back via Wakefield.

On a sunny day in 1980, No. 55002 *The King's Own Yorkshire Light Infantry* waits at Newcastle's platform 8 alongside the new order, which appears here in the shape of an HST set. No. 55002 is yet to surrender her BR blue livery to the pseudo two-tone green she later wore, but she appears to have recently lost a works plate.

In March 1980, No. 55014 *The Duke of Wellington's Regiment* is seen here on familiar territory at Newcastle's platform 10. This was our favourite spot, as it gave us a view across the Tyne to Gateshead's 'ash-heaps' and to trains on the King Edward VII Bridge. The structure projecting from the station's curtain wall was the bridge, which contained the relay room for the signal box. Each relay was contained in a large glass box like an aquarium.

The legendary Finsbury Park white cabs first brightened up BR's drab blue landscape in 1979 with No. 55003 *Meld*, and soon the other five remaining racehorses were similarly adorned. Sadly, No. 55001 *St. Paddy* and No. 55020 *Nimbus* were already gone. Here, No. 55018 *Ballymoss* speeds through Low Fell on the outskirts of Gateshead with 1S27, the Plymouth–Edinburgh service, on 26 April 1980. In the distance can be seen Tyne Yard's floodlight towers and the taller microwave communication mast.

An atmospheric monochrome shot of Newcastle Central's platform 9 in 1980, with the driver of No. 55004 *Queen's Own Highlander* leaning out of his window. Judging by the position of the train, this must be a short rake of Mk1s, so this is probably an Edinburgh 'stopper'. A BR Sulzer Class 45 or 46 'Peak' stands alongside in the centre road.

No. 55004 *Queen's Own Highlander* again, on a different day in 1980 – this time at Darlington Bank Top station with a southbound train. In front of the distinctive 1939 LNER-built Darlington South signal box, and hidden behind the locomotive, are the avoiding lines, which take a straight path outside the train shed and allow non-stop services to pass at speed.

Ian has captured No. 55014 *The Duke of Wellington's Regiment* at Newark North Gate with 1L41, the 10.05 King's Cross–York service on 10 August 1980. Later that day I travelled from York to King's Cross behind No. 55014 on 1A10 during my First Class Eastern Railrover. The previous night I completed 414 miles behind No. 40103 with 1S72 from London to Edinburgh, diverted via Lincoln, Knottingley, Stockton and the Blyth and Tyne. No. 55005 took me from Edinburgh back to York on 1V93. Happy days.

The white cabs and roof detail of No. 55003 *Meld* are seen to advantage through a broken window of the footbridge at York as she warms up in readiness to take over from the incoming Class 47 on 1S27, the 07.25 Plymouth–Edinburgh train on 15 August 1980. In these days of cross-country 'Voyager' units, it is hard to conceive of such locomotive changes taking place.

Peterborough station was extensively remodelled in the early 1970s to permit high-speed running for non-stop services. This perspective shot of No. 55016 *Gordon Highlander* in August 1980 emphasises how straight the platforms are now when compared to the reverse curves and speed restrictions that existed previously.

Seen at Doncaster on 16 August 1980, Nos 55011 *The Royal Northumberland Fusiliers* and 55013 *The Black Watch* are being hauled to York depot from Finsbury Park by No. 47430. No. 55011 ran minus a nameplate from June to September 1980. The holdall being wielded by the enthusiast on the right was one of several styles in favour. I preferred an old-fashioned haversack.

No. 55011 *The Royal Northumberland Fusiliers* is about to depart Hull Paragon with 1A18, the 12.34 to King's Cross on 16 August 1980. The driver allowed Ian a cab ride as far as Goole, then he continued 'on the cushions' to Peterborough. In the middle of August 1980, he combined Northumbrian, Yorkshire and East Midlands Ranger tickets to give him unlimited travel between Berwick and Peterborough, including the routes to Scarborough, Hull, Cleethorpes and Skegness.

A classic 1980 view of No. 55003 *Meld* pulling away from Newcastle with a rake of Mk1s, probably on an Edinburgh stopper. Ian has caught me in full flight in blue parka running alongside. When travelling on the stoppers, in those days I would listen endlessly to Blondie's *Parallel Lines* on an ancient cassette player and, to this day, whenever I hear 'Sunday Girl' or '11:59' I am instantly in an Mk1 compartment behind a white-cabbed Deltic.

While Finsbury Park's racehorses looked stylish with their white cabs, Gateshead's regiments, by now reallocated to York, could usually be recognised by their near-black appearance. Here, No. 55011 *The Royal Northumberland Fusiliers* is at rest at Haymarket depot, Edinburgh, in 1980. The massive bulk and 69-foot, six-inch length of the locomotive can be appreciated here.

Both to become railtour regulars, most famously on 2 January 1982, Nos 55015 *Tulyar* and 55022 *Royal Scots Grey* are captured side-by-side at Newcastle in 1980. A detail worthy of note is the commemorative plaque on the front of No. 55015, marking her participation in the Rainhill 150 event. Happily, both locomotives survive in preservation.

A typical enthusiast's view of Gateshead depot in 1980. No. 55003 *Meld* is in the company of fellow English Electrics in the shape of Nos 37077 and 40060, together with an example of the ubiquitous Class 08 shunter. A variety of architectural styles is evident, with vestiges of the original Greenesfield works on the right. While it was possible to look around most depots around the country by asking permission of the foreman, Gateshead was notoriously difficult to enter!

The nameplate of No. 55012 *Crepello*, photographed at Berwick in August 1980. Finsbury Park and Haymarket Deltics shared an identical typeface inside square-cornered nameplates, whereas Gateshead's allocation featured rounded corners and a narrower font. It was a nice touch by the Eastern Region's PR department to continue the LNER's proud tradition of bestowing racehorse names on its top link locomotives.

No. 55009 *Alycidon* accelerates around the curve at the south end of the King Edward VII Bridge, having left Newcastle and crossed the Tyne heading south in 1980. Before this bridge was built in 1906, Anglo-Scottish trains had to use Stephenson's High Level Bridge of 1849 and reverse at the Central station. The unique circular layout, with triangular junctions at the Gateshead end of each bridge, remains to this day and provides great flexibility of operation.

Nos 55018 *Ballymoss* and No. 55005 *The Price of Wales's Own Regiment of Yorkshire* at Newcastle in 1980. Note that both Deltics have twin windscreen wiper blades fitted. These began to be replaced by more reliable single wipers during the late 1970s, but Nos 55001/3/4/5/6/12/16/18/20, along with No. 55021 at one end only, retained twin wipers to the end.

Newcastle Central again in 1980, where Ian's favourite, No. 55012 *Crepello*, appears to have filled John Dobson's magnificent Victorian train shed with Deltic 'clag'. A Class 03 station pilot lurks in the 'wall-side' sidings. The 1849-built station fully merits its Grade I listed status and is nowadays beautifully restored, most notably in the sumptuous Centurion bar with its wonderful tiled walls.

80 miles south of Newcastle, the equally impressive York station plays host to No. 55012 *Crepello* and No. 55017 *The Durham Light Infantry* in 1980. No. 55017 is in the bay platform and is almost certainly on one of the London semi-fast stoppers. Above No. 55017 can be seen the city walls, through which an opening allowed rail access to the original terminus, much of which survives, although partly occupied by Hudson House, visible beyond the parapet of the wall.

A 1980 scene at Doncaster with No. 55009 *Alycidon* awaiting departure. Judging by the amount of dead insects on the yellow nose, this was probably taken in the summer. By 1982, the Deltic Preservation Society had raised sufficient funds to save not one but two Deltics from scrap, and No. 55009 was selected as the best of the surviving 'racehorses' to join sister No. 55019 in their new life at the North Yorkshire Moors Railway.

Another shot of the King Edward VII Bridge in 1980 as No. 55010 *The King's Own Scottish Borderer* gathers speed and heads south. The newly constructed Queen Elizabeth II Bridge can be seen behind, which carries the Metro over the Tyne between the tunnels below Newcastle and Gateshead. A classic car in the shape of a Hillman Hunter is parked lineside and the Newcastle skyline features the floodlights of what was then a quite archaic St James's Park.

A Deltic basher's view in 1980 as No. 55019 *Royal Highland Fusilier* slowly takes the sharp left curve out of Newcastle towards the King Edward VII Bridge for the south. The severe curves at both ends of the bridge meant a cautious departure from Newcastle, and it wasn't until the train had gained the straight in Bensham cutting that the driver could accelerate properly.

The south end of York station in 1980, where we see No. 55010 *The King's Own Scottish Borderer* making a spirited, characteristically smoky departure with a London service. Although Nos 55011 and 55018 also spent time minus a nameplate, No. 55010's was missing for the longest time, and I always thought it didn't look right. At least in the early 1960s, before they were named, they carried the BR crest in the centre to relieve the monotony of those long body sides.

A wintry 1980 scene at Newcastle as No. 55012 *Crepello* arrives from the north. The workman in a high-visibility vest on the lighting tower must have had a good view as the Deltic slid beneath his feet. The Federation Brewery building on the far right is now long gone, revealing a long, tall section of the mediaeval town wall, which had been incorporated into industrial buildings centuries earlier.

Newcastle's platform 8 in the snow of 1980; No. 55017 *The Durham Light Infantry* is awaiting 'the board' to set off for Scotland. No. 55017 was easily recognisable as she had the smallest of all of the regimental nameplates. The usual contingent of enthusiasts is hanging around. I wonder where they all are now?

In 1980, Newcastle-upon-Tyne celebrated its 900th anniversary. The Romans knew it as Pons Aelius; then it became Monkchester until William, son of the Conqueror, built his new castle here. Victorian railway mania had little respect for history and the Newcastle & Berwick Railway's main line bisected the castle. The famous keep is visible beyond No. 55019 *Royal Highland Fusilier* as she arrives from the north.

Newcastle in 1980; young enthusiasts are practising the ancient art of nameplate rubbing with wax crayons on No. 55004 *Queen's Own Highlander*. There was a decorating shop near the Central station, whose staff must have thought it odd, scruffy boys buying odd rolls of wallpaper, one at a time. *Meld* was easy but *The Prince of Wales's Own Regiment of Yorkshire* was a challenge. I remember an irate station supervisor shouting at a couple of boys desperately finishing their rubbing as a Deltic began to pull away from the platform!

An unusual low-angle 1980 shot of No. 55004 *Queen's Own Highlander* coming off the King Edward VII Bridge. The train is curving west to take the main line towards Durham, while the route to the right heads east past Gateshead shed towards Sunderland and the Durham coast. The Scottish & Newcastle Brewery dominates the skyline to the right of the train, now sadly no more, taking its heady aroma with it.

Platform 8 at Newcastle again. On this fine day in 1980 its occupant was No. 55021 *Argyll & Sutherland Highlander*. Although they perhaps lacked the mystery of the Finsbury Park racehorse names, the Gateshead and Haymarket regimental names were impressive and dignified, unlike many of the names inflicted on modern locomotives.

In my childhood, the bridge that carries Smithy Lane across the main line and the northern throat of Tyne Yard was another favourite spot of mine and my dad's when watching the trains. I have faint memories of seeing a long line of Clayton Class 17s out of use at the back of the yard. They were long gone by 1980 when No. 55006 *The Fife & Forfar Yeomanry* was captured at speed with an Up express.

First of the class, No. 55022 *Royal Scots Grey* began life as D9000 and, while her twenty-one sisters retained their numerical identities when renumbered under the TOPS system, 9000 became No. 55022 as 55000 would not have been a valid number. Hardly anyone in enthusiast circles referred to 'Class 55'. They were always 'Deltics'. Here she is arriving at York in 1980 from the south with the imposing Holgate Bridge in the distance.

Another 1980 photograph of No. 55012 *Crepello* storming out of platform 10 at Newcastle Central. I thought it a shame when the remaining Deltics were concentrated at York depot and the racehorses lost their Finsbury Park white cabs. No. 55012 was withdrawn the following May still wearing hers.

A pleasing symmetry at Newcastle in 1980 as No. 55004 *Queen's Own Highlander* and No. 55018 *Ballymoss* stand at platforms 10 and 9 respectively. The spotters' equipment includes a camera and a roll of wallpaper. Back then, a cup of Maxpax tea from a train buffet cost 19p and station platforms were thronged with teenage boys in parkas sitting on 'Brute' parcels barrows like that in the foreground here.

No. 55018 *Ballymoss* looking good next to one of her successors in the sun at Newcastle's platform 8 in 1980. We tended to ignore the HSTs, in much the same way that our predecessors on the platform would have disregarded the diesels that replaced their beloved Pacifics and V2s. Time has proven, however, the HSTs were a wise investment and even I have to admit they have given sterling service for almost four decades now.

No. 55010 *The King's Own Scottish Borderer* arrives in platform 8 at Newcastle Central in 1980. This locomotive was famously the first of the fleet to reach an astonishing 2 million miles after only twelve years of service, an average of approximately 450 miles per day. Note the small circular ventilator close to the horn. These were fitted during 1976/7 to all Deltics except Nos 55008/9/15/20/22.

Finsbury Park depot's white cabs shine through the workaday grime of No. 55009 *Alycidon* as she pauses at Newcastle Central sometime in 1980. The racehorse Alycidon was descended from Hyperion, after which one of Gresley's A3 Pacifics was named, and he was also the sire of Meld.

Another day in 1980, and this unusual shot sees No. 55021 *Argyll & Sutherland Highlander* arriving at Berwick-upon-Tweed from the south. As at Newcastle, Berwick's heritage was the victim of railway mania as the station occupies most of the site of the mediaeval castle and only a section of curtain wall remains, seen in the background here. Beyond, it slopes steeply down to the Tweed beside Stephenson's Royal Border Bridge.

No. 55012 *Crepello* waits at the south end of York station in 1980. The enthusiasts on the left display some interesting fashions, while the behaviour of the photographer who has descended the platform ramp on the right would not be tolerated on today's railway. The racehorse after which she was named was a Derby winner, ridden by the legendary Lester Piggott, beating Ballymoss in the process.

A fine monochrome study by Ian of No. 55013 *The Black Watch* at Newcastle Central's platform 10 in 1980. Whenever I think about No. 55013, I am taken back to an evening on an Eastern Railrover when the main line was under flood water somewhere near Retford and No. '13 charged right through it, creating a huge wash, with water coming in through the carriage doors. Not sure the Deltics were designed to be amphibious.

No. 55021 *Argyll & Sutherland Highlander* leaves Newcastle Central around 1980. She is almost certainly about to curve sharply left onto the King Edward VII Bridge. The route that curves right was at that time the main route to Carlisle via the Scotswood Bridge. This closed in 1982, since when Carlisle services have travelled via Dunston.

No. 55011 *The Royal Northumberland Fusiliers* stands at platform 8 in Newcastle Central station sometime around 1980. No. 55011 was another of my favourites, being named after the county of my birth. Ironically it was in that county, on the infamous Morpeth curve in 1969, that she was driven too fast on the 'Night Aberdonian', causing the derailment of all vehicles apart from the locomotive, and the deaths of six people.

No. 55022 *Royal Scots Grey* moves off in response to the 'double yellow' signal at Newcastle Central on a murky winter's day in 1980. She is possibly heading for the High Level Bridge, to the right of the castle keep, to make for Gateshead sheds. No. '22 possessed a unique front footstep at each end, above the buffer beams, a relic of the experimental flashing headlamp she carried when new.

The marker lights of No. 55019 *Royal Highland Fusilier* pierce the gathering evening gloom at platform 8 in Newcastle Central station in 1980. Purchased two years later by the Deltic Preservation Society for the princely sum of £16,550, she has since operated in thirty-three out of her thirty-four years in preservation – a bargain indeed and testimony to the dedicated volunteers who look after her.

The blanked-off front footstep and short regimental nameplate tell us without looking at the number that it's No. 55017 *The Durham Light Infantry* occupying the centre road between platforms 14 and 15 at York. She is undoubtedly waiting to take over the Plymouth–Edinburgh service, 1S27, from an incoming 'Duff'.

An impressive close-up of Finsbury Park favourite No. 55018 *Ballymoss*, looking rather smart as she stands at platform 9 of Newcastle Central. The all-over yellow livery applied to each end since the late 1960s accentuates the bulbous shape of the Deltics. If I close my eyes I can still imagine the noise and vibration created by the twin idling Napier Deltic engines under Newcastle's cavernous overall roof.

No. 55022 *Royal Scots Grey* leaves platform 8 at Newcastle for the north, sometime in 1980. This unusual view was taken from the end of platform 4, one of the bays that served North and South Tyneside suburban services before the Metro opened, as well as the coast line to Sunderland and Teesside. No. 55022 was one of three Deltics never to receive the yellow plated-over headcode panels, along with Nos 55008 and 55020.

For a white-cabbed Finsbury Park 'racehorse', No. 55007 *Pinza* looks a little shabby here in 1980 at platform 9 in Newcastle Central station, which looks equally unkempt. Today John Dobson's masterpiece is beautifully cleaned and restored, with many of the insensitive alterations of the twentieth century removed and damage repaired. Most recently the portico, which used to be choked with taxi fumes, has been glazed and pedestrianised, making a much more pleasant environment.

No. 55005 *The Prince of Wales's Own Regiment of Yorkshire* at Newcastle's platform 8 in 1980. There are the usual Metro-Cammell DMUs in some of the bay platforms. These could have been on services to Sunderland, Middlesbrough or South Shields. The North Tyneside services had ceased in August 1980, when the first section of the Tyne & Wear Metro opened between the new underground station at Haymarket and the 1882 NER station at Tynemouth.

December 1980 at York. No. 55002 *The King's Own Yorkshire Light Infantry* has achieved instant celebrity status by sporting a version of its original two-tone green livery, sponsored by the National Railway Museum, which had earmarked her for preservation. At that time, we could not have dreamed that there would be five other survivors!

No. 55006 *The Fife & Forfar Yeomanry* stands at Newcastle's platform 8 in December 1980. No. 55006 was relatively elusive for me, as I only recorded four trips totalling 410 miles behind her, almost my lowest total apart from Nos 55001 and 55020. Her steam heating appears to be in working order as a solitary spotter sits on a parcels barrow next to his holdall. Two months later, No. 55006 would be withdrawn from service.

No. 55003 *Meld* arrives at Newcastle with empty coaching stock from Heaton on 20 December 1980. The loco was sadly withdrawn a few days later, becoming the third member of the class to be silenced forever. She will always be remembered as the first of the Finsbury Park 'white cabs'. The racehorse, Meld, after which the Deltic was named, was the only filly out of the eight Finsbury Park stablemates.

A last look at No. 55003 *Meld* as she is about to be removed from her last ever train, 1S27 at Newcastle, 29 December 1980. The locomotive proceeded light engine to York MPD where she was officially withdrawn from service the following day. She was originally due to work the final 'Hull Executive' before her planned withdrawal on 4 January 1981 but, with one power unit defective, the other one suspect and having a non-operational steam-heat boiler, the decision was made to withdraw early.

Following the demise of *Meld*, No. 55007 *Pinza* got dressed up for the occasion to work the last loco-hauled 'Hull Executive', 1D04, the 17.05 King's Cross–Hull on 3 January 1981. Here she is at the London terminus before departure. This service was famously the fastest loco-hauled train in the country at that time, being scheduled to average 91.4 mph from London to its first stop at Retford.

Looking resplendent in the snow at Newcastle Central is No. 55005 *The Prince of Wales's Own Regiment of Yorkshire* in the winter of 1980/81. She had received silver radiator grilles and red buffer beams in November 1980 when chosen to work a commemorative train to mark 150 years of Royal Mail by rail. Appearances can be deceptive, however, and, in February 1981, she and No. 55006 became the fourth and fifth Deltics to be withdrawn from service.

The winter sun shines on the battered body side of No. 55016 *Gordon Highlander* at York while it waits to relieve the loco on the incoming 1S27 Plymouth–Edinburgh train on 24 January 1981. No. 55016 was the only Deltic to retain the larger BR 'undecided arrow', her sisters having had them replaced with the smaller symbol during the 1970s. Like No. 55004, there had been a time when No. 55016's future was uncertain as she languished in Doncaster Works from January to September 1979. Remarkably, she is still with us today in preservation.

It is Valentine's Day in 1981 and, while many teenagers would have been more concerned with conventional affairs of the heart, our attention was focused on No. 55015 *Tulyar* at Darlington Bank Top with 1V93, the 09.50 Edinburgh–Plymouth, which she will take as far as York. Thirty-five years later, and *Tulyar* is nearing the end of a lengthy and thorough overhaul by the DPS at their Barrow Hill facility, which is well worth a visit.

The secondman of No. 55018 *Ballymoss* leans out awaiting the all-clear at Berwick-upon-Tweed on 11 April 1981 with 1S08, the 07.05 Newcastle–Edinburgh stopper. In a couple of miles she will cross the border into Scotland at Marshall Meadows. With their short rakes of Mk1 coaches and their frequent stops at remote outposts such as Acklington and Chathill, the Deltics were able to show off their superb acceleration on these services.

No. 55007 *Pinza*, with a steam-heating boiler doing its job, stands awaiting the whistle at Dunbar while working 1S14, the 08.10 Newcastle–Edinburgh on 15 April 1981. From here No. 55021 provided haulage south to Newcastle on 1V93, the 09.50 Edinburgh–Plymouth. I can still bring to mind that nostalgic smell of steam-heated Mk1s to this day. So much more organic than today's sterile all-electric railway.

No. 55013 *The Black Watch* erupts into life in the centre road at York on 17 April 1981, and is about to take over 1S27, the 07.25 Plymouth–Edinburgh, having worked the southbound equivalent, 1V93, that morning. Later that night she would take the 'Night Aberdonian' from Edinburgh Waverley to London King's Cross. I loved travelling on those overnight trains and we would do our best to claim a compartment for ourselves in those dimly lit steam-heated Mk1s.

The driver looks back from the cab of No. 55015 *Tulyar* at Alnmouth, looking for the green flag as she heads 1E08, the 07.18 Edinburgh–Newcastle stopper, on 20 April 1981. No. 55015 would be back in Edinburgh that evening to take an overnight to King's Cross. Hopefully, sometime soon, Alnmouth will once again be a junction station, as the Aln Valley Railway plans to reopen most of the Alnwick branch. Alnwick's superb station survives as an excellent second-hand bookshop.

By this time, railtours were becoming a regular occurrence. On 25 April 1981 the Deltic Preservation Society ran 'The North Briton' from York to Edinburgh and back. It was scheduled to travel via the Settle–Carlisle line but Pennine snow caused the train to be diverted via 'the other' Clapham Junction and Carnforth. All of this was behind No. 55002, but it was sister No. 55008 *The Green Howards* that brought the empty stock into York that morning.

Having arrived in Edinburgh with 'The North Briton' railtour via Carnforth, Shap and Beattock, No. 55002 *The King's Own Yorkshire Light Infantry* was bizarrely employed later that day at Waverley for some shunting involving a Craven's DMU car, despite there being a Class 08 station pilot alongside!

In 1981, before Gateshead had an allocation of Class 56s, we see Romanian-built No. 56027 alongside one of Gateshead's own Deltics, No. 55008 *The Green Howards*, by now reallocated to York. This was probably the cleanest she had been for years. No. 55008's black headcode panel and low-slung nameplate with the regimental crest above made her immediately recognisable.

Also in 1981, No. 55008 *The Green Howards* is seen setting off from York, about to pass under Holgate Bridge with a London stopper. At this time services still took the old main line at Chaloner's Whin Junction and ran to Doncaster via Selby and its swing bridge. Two years later this line closed due to potential mining subsidence and, if you pass Chaloner's Whin today, you would hardly know there had been a junction there.

No. 55014 *The Duke of Wellington's Regiment* leaves Manors with the early-morning stopping service 1S08, the 07.05 Newcastle–Edinburgh, on 30 May 1981. Manors was a large junction station immediately east of Newcastle. To the right of the Deltic can be seen the redundant buildings of Manors North, which was the part of the station used by North Tyneside loop trains to the coast via Jesmond and Benton.

A moment later, No. 55014 looks rather battle-weary as she accelerates away from Manors towards Heaton with 1S08. The leading vehicle is a BR Mk1 General Utility Van, or GUV. Alongside the main line at this point today, the Tyne & Wear Metro burrows underground as it heads under the city centre from Byker into Manors, Monument and St James.

June 1981 at Newcastle, and No. 55016 *Gordon Highlander* and a Stratford silver-roofed 'duff' stand beneath the curved roof. The Metro-Cammell DMUs in platform 7 display two different liveries that had replaced the drab overall blue of the 1970s. The unit furthest to the right wears the short-lived 'refurbished' colours, while the one nearest the buffer-stops is in the standard coaching stock blue and grey.

In the sunshine of 22 June 1981, No. 55016 *Gordon Highlander* stands at Newcastle with 1S12, the 05.50 King's Cross–Aberdeen. She worked this as far as Edinburgh, and then hauled a later service to Aberdeen before working 1E48 'The Night Aberdonian' service to King's Cross throughout. All in a day's work for a Deltic. Thanks to the excellent Napier Chronicles website for the details.

A spectacular capture of No. 55022 *Royal Scots Grey* providing a composition of exhaust and train-heat steam at Newcastle in 1981 as she departs from platform 8 with an Edinburgh stopper. Thanks to the Deltic 9000 Fund, the doyen of the class No. 55022 became the fourth Deltic to be saved from the cutter's torch, following No. 55002 at the National Railway Museum and Nos 55009/55019 by the Deltic Preservation Society.

The curve of Newcastle's platform 10 is plain to see as No. 55014 *The Duke of Wellington's Regiment* brings the stock of an Edinburgh stopper in, sometime in 1981. A travelling post office vehicle brings up the rear of her train. No. 03094 is busy with a bogie wagon in the 'wall-side' sidings. The North Eastern Railway water tower in the left distance dates from 1891 and remains there to this day.

In fading light, No. 55008 *The Green Howards* is surrounded by DMUs at Newcastle in 1981. In my opinion, the Deltics looked so much better without the yellow plated-over headcode panels. No. 55008 lasted in service to the very end of 1981, and was scrapped in August 1982. One cab was preserved and can now be seen at Barrow Hill, along with one from No. 55021.

A standard Newcastle Central platform 10 shot of No. 55019 *Royal Highland Fusilier*, taken in 1981. As D9019, she was the last Deltic to receive nameplates at a ceremony at Glasgow Central in 1965, having run for more than three years unnamed. No. 55019 was to become a celebrity in 1982 when she was selected for preservation by the Deltic Preservation Society.

Darlington Bank Top on 22 June 1981 sees No. 55022 *Royal Scots Grey* on 1E10, the 09.10 Dundee–King's Cross, which she worked from Edinburgh. Having travelled behind 'number 22' from Newcastle to Darlington, I waited for No. 55010 back home again on the northbound equivalent, 1S76. Visible at the top left is the microwave communication mast, which provided a link between those at Tyne Yard and York's magnificent ex-North Eastern Railway headquarters building.

It is 27 June 1981 and No. 55010 *The King's Own Scottish Borderer* awaits departure from Edinburgh Waverley with 1E35, the 20.45 service to King's Cross. A BRCW Class 27 can be seen beyond. No. 55010 had worked from the English to the Scottish capital that morning on 1S12. I rode with her as far as Newcastle, having travelled north in the morning behind No. 40007 on 1S08, in order to attend an open day at Glasgow's St. Rollox works.

On 4 July 1981 at Newcastle, No. 55018 *Ballymoss* is one of only four 'racehorses' still in service, *Crepello* having been withdrawn in May and joining *Meld*, *St. Paddy* and *Nimbus* in oblivion. Those remaining had also sadly lost their trademark white cabs. Here, *Ballymoss* heads 1A39, the 10.50 Newcastle–King's Cross, restricted to one power unit only. She would last in service until October 1981.

One week later, at Newcastle again, and another 'racehorse', this time my favourite, No. 55007 *Pinza*, waits for the off at platform 8 on 11 July 1981 with 1S27, the 07.36 Plymouth–Edinburgh, which she took over at York. The bay platforms beyond see a Metro-Cammell DMU either arriving or departing.

A study of No. 55007's nameplate at Newcastle, as she awaits departure with 1S27 for Edinburgh. The fuel gauge indicating the 900-gallon capacity can be seen on the underslung tanks. I always liked the neatness of the Finsbury Park racehorse names, and I used to possess a good full-sized replica of a *Pinza* nameplate, handmade by a friend who was a pattern maker by trade. I later donated it to the DPS for fundraising purposes.

An unusual working for a Deltic on 25 July 1981, as No. 55010 *The King's Own Scottish Borderer* is seen here at Newcastle on 1S98, the 14.35 Scarborough–Glasgow train, which she worked as far as Edinburgh. She had gone that morning light engine from York to the coast to pick up the train at its starting point. This was perhaps a running-in turn as she had just received a 'B' exam at York.

No. 55010 has the 'double yellow' and leaves Newcastle with 1S98, the 14.35 Scarborough–Glasgow train, passing No. 37072, which had assisted No. 40022 into Newcastle with a northbound train. No. 55010 must have been in good shape following her 'B' exam as that night she took an overnight service from Edinburgh to King's Cross.

By this time in July 1981, I was employed as a student technician engineer in the Signalling and Telecommunications department at Forth Banks, Newcastle, and had to attend an induction course at Hudson House in York. Lunch breaks gave me opportunities to grab photos of Deltics and here we see No. 55009 *Alycidon* heading north past York depot, where a Class 25 awaits its next turn. The distinctive shape of York Minster looms on the horizon.

The footbridge over Leeman Road in York provides a great vantage point and, in July 1981, No. 55013 *The Black Watch* is making a smoky departure from platform 14. If anything, the overall roof at York is possibly even more spectacular than that at Newcastle, although it was built almost thirty years later. Almost as fascinating is the array of cars on display, including a Morris Marina and a Vauxhall Viva.

The same location on another July day in 1981, and this time it is No. 55014 *The Duke of Wellington's Regiment* filling the skies of York with her pungent exhaust. On the left can be seen the distant chimneys of the old NER Headquarters building, with the Royal Station Hotel looming over the Scarborough bay platforms, which contain the usual DMUs, including a BRCW 'Calder Valley' set.

The last of the Deltics to enter service, in 1962, and still looking smart in July 1981, is No. 55021 *Argyll & Sutherland Highlander* as she enters York from the north. Today's selection in the car park includes a Datsun Cherry, Renault 12 and a Triumph Toledo. I wonder how their mileages compared to the millions accumulated by No. 55021?

On 29 July 1981 No. 55017 *The Durham Light Infantry* brings 1E29 into Peterborough. To most of the population, this was the day of a royal wedding. The Eastern Region, brilliantly seizing the opportunity, offered £2 travel anywhere within the region except London for those who wanted to avoid it. My mates and I took advantage of this, venturing into deepest East Anglia on Class 37s, having caught No. 55021 from Newcastle to Peterborough overnight.

Another clever ER initiative was to run two Merrymaker excursions from Newcastle down the Esk Valley line to Whitby on 2 and 30 of August 1981. Both featured No. 55002 *The King's Own Yorkshire Light Infantry* and offered hitherto unknown photograph opportunities, such as the one here at Grosmont with the green Deltic alongside matching Beyer-Peacock 'Hymek' diesel-hydraulic D7029 owned by the Diesel Traction Group.

Also in August 1981, No. 55002 is seen in the unfamiliar surroundings of Whitby Town after arrival. The lad on the right is in a hurry, either to get a photograph or to sample one of Whitby's excellent chippies. BR rather short-sightedly lifted all but one track in the station some years after this but, now that the North Yorkshire Moors Railway runs regular services from Pickering through to Whitby, the run-around facility has been reinstated.

The journey from Middlesbrough to Whitby entails a reversal at Battersby Junction, a railway gem in the middle of nowhere. On those sunny August days in 1981, any 'normal' Merrymaker passengers on the train must have thought the world had gone mad, as dozens of enthusiasts spilled out of the coaching stock and all over the track to take photos of No. 55002 as she ran around the train – a scene that is unimaginable today.

Pictured is the remote North Yorkshire outpost of Battersby, again in August 1981, with No. 55002 *The King's Own Yorkshire Light Infantry* about to set back onto the Merrymaker stock. As well as the present day Esk Valley routes to Middlesbrough and Whitby, both of which approach from the north into what is now a terminus, Battersby Junction once boasted routes west to Picton, and south-east climbing steeply into the hills to ironstone workings that fed the great iron and steel industry of Teesside.

No. 55004 *Queen's Own Highlander* arrives at Berwick with 1E10, the 09.10 Dundee–King's Cross on 14 August 1981. This was a summer-only service, if I remember correctly, and gave us another option for long-distance Deltic haulage on top of the 1S12/1E26 and 1V93/1S27 diagrams.

On 2 September 1981 at York depot, No. 55018 *Ballymoss* is stabled with Brush products Nos 47480 and 31319. It could be argued that both of these types were more successful than the more glamorous Deltics, but the entire 263-strong Brush Type 2 fleet had to be re-engined with English Electric power units in the late 1960s following reliability problems with their original Mirrlees engines.

September gave way to October and time was running out for our beloved Deltics. Frequent railtours were taking the locomotives to some quite exotic locations. The 'Wessex Deltic' ran on 17 October 1981, and No. 55015 *Tulyar*, white cabs restored, took me from Finsbury Park along the North London line to Clapham Junction and Bournemouth, stopping off at Eastleigh depot and Portsmouth Harbour on the way back. Here No. 55015 is seen with No. 33027 and at Eastleigh, as a train load of enthusiasts wander about. I presume the authorities had isolated the electrified third rails.

While I was on the south coast, Ian was headed for Aberdeen, also on 17 October 1981. This was a Merrymaker excursion worked by No. 55009 _Alycidon_ from Newcastle as far as Perth where Nos 27029 and 27037 took the train forward to Inverness. Here is an immaculately turned-out No. 55009 at Newcastle in the early hours, prior to departure.

The Merrymaker continued from Inverness with No. 40167 on the eastbound leg to Aberdeen. Meanwhile, the Deltic had travelled light engine from Perth to Aberdeen to bring the train back to Newcastle. No. 55009 _Alycidon_ looks as good as new as she is framed by the signal gantry at the south end of Aberdeen station.

On 20 October 1981, No. 55002 *The King's Own Yorkshire Light Infantry* is captured at Stalybridge on 1M62, the 08.50 York–Liverpool on a proving run after failing with loss of power a few days earlier. This turn was popular for test runs with travelling fitters. With the remaining fleet now concentrated at York depot, the Deltics became a regular choice for such Trans-Pennine diagrams.

Having left Stalybridge and the Pennines behind her, No. 55002 has arrived at Manchester Victoria. At the time, this seemed to be one of the grottiest stations on the BR network. It was the Lancashire & Yorkshire Railway's main station in the city and, unusually, it joined end-on with the London & North Western's Manchester Exchange, sharing Europe's longest platform.

No. 55002 waits in an eerily quiet Liverpool Lime Street with 1E99, the 13.05 Liverpool–York service on the same day. During the month of October, the green Deltic was stabled at York depot, working to Liverpool three times and hauling two railtours, namely 'The Two Firths Express' on 10 October and 'The Celtic Deltic' on 31 October.

No. 55021 *Argyll & Sutherland Highlander* is pictured on the Tyne Valley line at Hexham with 1M04, the 07.18 Edinburgh–Carlisle service via Newcastle, on 21 October 1981. Note the unique design of top headboard bracket, which differs slightly from that fitted to every other member of the class. This service was an extension to the Edinburgh–Newcastle stoppers seen earlier in the book.

A week after No. 55015 *Tulyar* had taken me from London to the south coast and back, here she is arriving in Newcastle's platform 8 with the DPS's 'Deltic Salute' railtour to Aberdeen on 24 October 1981. DPS fundraising was in full swing as withdrawal approached, and I had organised several fundraising events in Newcastle. A couple of years later, I even hired a Tyne & Wear PTE double-decker bus to take a load of us from Newcastle to Pickering for a Deltic running day on the NYMR.

Tulyar has paused at Montrose en route to Aberdeen with the 'Deltic Salute' and, as usual, a trainload of enthusiasts has spilled down the platform ramp. Nobody seemed to mind in those days and I don't recall ever seeing anyone coming close to being hit by a train. I think I preferred the workmanlike appearance of a typical Gateshead Deltic to one all dressed up like this, with white pipes, headboard and wreath.

An unusual angle taken from Newcastle's Castle Keep of No. 55002 *The King's Own Yorkshire Light Infantry* at the head of 'The Celtic Deltic' railtour on 31 October 1981. As she heads east towards Heaton Junction before taking the main line north to Edinburgh, she will cross the spectacular 80-foot-high Dean Street arch and the five-arched Ouseburn viaduct.

Here we see one of Tyneside's favourites and, as was often the case, No. 55017 *The Durham Light Infantry* is absolutely covered in muck as she enters platform 9 at Newcastle off the King Edward VII Bridge in late 1981. The DLI name had previously been used on Gresley ex-LNER V2 No. 60964, although she had only been named in 1958.

My favourite, No. 55007 *Pinza*, looks fantastic in Ian's shot here of her in the snow at Gateshead in December 1981. No. 55007 was withdrawn on 31 December along with all of her sisters except Nos 55002, 55009, 55015 and 55022. These last four, of course, all survive to this day in preservation. I have always regretted that *Pinza* was not to be so fortunate.

Twelve days before the end, No. 55010 *The King's Own Scottish Borderer* is still smoking and steaming as she stands at Darlington Bank Top at the head of 1M73, the 11.21 Newcastle–Liverpool service on 19 December 1981. She had been restricted to one engine since 12 December after No. 2 engine, Power Unit No. 454, failed with a suspected fractured liner. Note the small circular disc on the nose end. Nos 55010, 55019 and 55021 had these fitted in the mid-1960s to allow a communication system to be fitted if hauling the royal train.

It is Christmas Eve 1981, one week before withdrawal for all Deltics apart from those selected for the 2 January farewell tour. It was a cold bleak end to the year and, here in the snow at Newcastle, No. 55017 *The Durham Light Infantry* brings some seasonal cheer to local enthusiasts on 1S12, the 05.50 King's Cross–Aberdeen, which she worked throughout before returning to York on 1E26.

On a cold Tuesday 29 December 1981, No. 55021 *Argyll & Sutherland Highlander* powers out of Darlington past milepost 44, working 1E52, the 09.10 Dundee–King's Cross. This was the last run Ian had behind this fine machine as, two days later, she was switched off forever. She is in a very dirty condition and restricted to one engine only, as power unit No. 445 had fractured a cylinder liner while working an Aberdeen train on 8 December. Amazingly, No. 55021 continued in service until the final day with this restriction.

No. 55019 *Royal Highland Fusilier* is at Newcastle on the very last morning of Deltic-hauled service trains, 31 December 1981, with 1S14, the 08.10 to Edinburgh; it had been restricted to one engine since 16 December due to a burst radiator. Ian's moves were to Alnmouth on No. 55019 for No. 47121 back to Newcastle on 1M04 for No. 55022 north to Berwick on 1S12. Then a HST to York for No. 55015 on the 15.50 to King's Cross, which he did to Newark, where he said his farewells as No. 55015 departed into the darkness. The only other Deltics to work that final day were Nos 55017 and 55021.

The first production Deltic, No. 55022 *Royal Scots Grey*, on her last BR service train, 1S12, the 05.50 King's Cross–Aberdeen, which she would work as far as Edinburgh. This is New Year's Eve 1981 again, and she is seen here at Berwick upon Tweed, waiting for the 'off'. Haymarket depot would set to work preparing her for her big day two days later on the 'Deltic Scotsman Farewell'.

Ian's last BR Deltic-hauled service train was No. 55015 *Tulyar* on 1A26, the 15.50 York–King's Cross on 31 December 1981. This is at York before departure. Ian 'bailed' at Newark, where he caught an HST home to Newcastle. He was still only fourteen years old. I cannot imagine today allowing my fourteen-year-old son to do all the things we used to get up to!

An uncharacteristically grimy No. 55009 *Alycidon* has the dubious honour of acting as standby locomotive for the 'Deltic Scotsman Farewell' on 2 January 1982. She is seen here at Newcastle wearing the classic 1960s 'winged thistle' headboard that was specially designed for the Deltic-hauled 'Flying Scotsman' – a very nice touch by whoever thought of putting it there.

As 1981 came to a gloomy, wintry close, time was finally called on the remaining Deltic squadron and everyone who couldn't get a ticket on the 'Deltic Scotsman Farewell' on 2 January 1982 was somewhere lineside to catch a last tearful look at No. 55015 northbound and No. 55022 on the return to London. No. 55015 *Tulyar*, white cabs once again restored, stands on the avoiding lines at Newcastle.

2 January 1982 at Newcastle, and the 'Deltic Scotsman Farewell' sets off for Edinburgh behind No. 55015 *Tulyar*. Later that day, in the gathering gloom, the train returned to King's Cross with No. 55022 *Royal Scots Grey* in charge. Her arrival at the London terminus was recorded for posterity on national television; thousands turned out to see her arrival and the last four Deltics were officially withdrawn. It was the end of an era.

Thousands of Deltic fans flocked to Doncaster Works on 27 February 1982 to take a last look at those locomotives that had not yet met their oxyacetylene-fuelled fate. Among the once-proud machines on display was No. 55004 *Queen's Own Highlander*, now looking quite sorry for herself, bereft of nameplates and with corrosion visibly taking hold. No. 55004 has the grim distinction of being the last of the class to be scrapped, in July 1983.

The two months that have elapsed since Ian's December 1981 shot at Gateshead have not been kind to No. 55007 *Pinza* as she is surrounded by admirers at Doncaster. We were all very glad to be given this opportunity by BREL to pay our last respects to our favourites, although some cynics labelled it as nothing more than a moneymaking scheme at the time.

This slightly happier sight on 27 February 1982 shows No. 55022 *Royal Scots Grey* among the crowds at Doncaster. She appears hardly any different to her service days. She happily left Doncaster in September 1983 for the Nene Valley Railway, having been saved by the Deltic 9000 Fund. Those parkas with the furry hoods are back in fashion again today!

It would be five months later when I next visited Doncaster on an official Deltic Preservation Society visit to view our new purchases, Nos 55009 and 55019. This was 24 July 1982 and we were greeted with the grisly sight of this line of eight Deltics, headed by No. 55004 *Queen's Own Highlander*. Not all of the eight were headed for oblivion, however, for immediately beyond No. 55004 is pioneer No. 55022, which departed for pastures new the following year.

On the same day, my beloved No. 55007 *Pinza* was in an advanced state of dismantling, as can be seen here. The remains of her two cabs are in the foreground, and her roofless main frames and body sides lie beyond. One of her grey control cabinets can be seen where it would have separated the cab from the engine room and, to its left, is part of a traction motor blower, which would have been in the nose end.

A closer view of one of No. 55007's cabs, poignantly grounded next to two canisters of the dreaded oxyacetylene, which fuelled the instruments of her demise. The open wagons beyond would be used to take away the scrap. Two-and-a-half years prior to this, I had witnessed No. 55020 *Nimbus* in a similar state, with No. 55001 *St. Paddy* looking on, but my Kodak Instamatic could not cope in the fading January light and the photographs I took were hopeless.

I was back at Doncaster on 20 August 1982 for the happy occasion of the official handover of No. 55009 *Alycidon* and No. 55019 *Royal Highland Fusilier* to the Deltic Preservation Society. Both locomotives had been restored to working order and repainted, with replica nameplates and works plates. It was quite a feeling to be part of this piece of history, having been an active fundraiser and local organiser, and here I was as a stakeholder in these two pieces of complex engineering. I was aged just eighteen.

The dawn of a new era, as a privately owned Deltic is about to work a train on a preserved railway for the first time. It is 21 August 1982 and No. 55009 *Alycidon* and No. 55019 *Royal Highland Fusilier* stand side-by-side at Grosmont station on the North Yorkshire Moors Railway. No. 55019 did the first 36-mile round trip to Pickering, followed by No. 55009. Ian interrupted his All-line Railrover to be there that day.

We signed up as trainee firemen on the NYMR and became active DPS volunteers on 'our' locomotives. As trainee secondmen, we were occasionally rostered on the footplate, which was a dream come true. This was 30 August 1983, and I took this shot from the cab of No. 55019 as she was about to pass No. 55009, with Ian in her cab, at Levisham. On one winter's day in 1983, we received instructions to prepare one of the Deltics for traffic at short notice, which meant priming and barring over the power units by hand before starting up for the driver. Such responsibility!

We were part of a working party tasked with wire-brushing, priming and glossing the Deltics' bogies. In retrospect, we possibly got a bit carried away picking out the various valves and hoses in different colours! Here is No. 55019 *Royal Highland Fusilier* at Grosmont shed in about 1983. When working for the railway, we tended to sleep on the floor in the station house at Grosmont but, if it was DPS work, we would sleep in their Mk1 BSK up the headshunt.

No. 55009 *Alycidon* looks wonderful as she threads her way through the glaciated valley of Newtondale Gorge between Goathland and Levisham, in about 1984. The fifth coach is an example of BR's experimental XP64 stock, which heralded the blue and grey era, and behind that are some Mk1 Pullman cars, used on the fantastic NYMR dining service, which is heartily recommended!

No. 55009 *Alycidon* passes the derelict Newtondale signal box *c.* 1984. The 24-mile journey from Pickering to Whitby is well worth doing. Most of the route was engineering by George Stephenson and the first section opened in 1835. It included a rope-hauled incline from Beck Hole to Goathland, which was superseded by the 'Deviation' route in 1865.

No. 55019 *Royal Highland Fusilier*, also in about 1984 in Newtondale, looks a little out of place with a short rake of 'blood and custards'. I should point out that these shots were made possible by the possession of an official lineside photographer's pass and the wearing of a high-visibility vest. This is essential if such photography is to be attempted. Note the distinctive NER half-milepost on the right.

An immaculate No. 55019 *Royal Highland Fusilier* has been putting her 3,300 horse power to use on a permanent way train as she passes Grosmont shed on 26 April 1984. She has just descended the 3 miles of 1 in 49 incline from Goathland, which is a serious challenge to any form of traction in the other direction.

At a Doncaster works open day on 27 July 1984, it was obvious that the Deltic 9000 people had been busy with their first purchase since she left Doncaster the previous year, and No. 55022 looked splendid as No. 9000 *Royal Scots Grey*. Like No. 55019, No. 9000 has been fitted with replica regimental crests above her nameplates. A queue of enthusiasts is patiently waiting to 'cab' her.

The first preservation home of No. 9000 *Royal Scots Grey* was the Nene Valley Railway near Peterborough. Here she is on an appropriate rake of coaching stock at Wansford station around 1984. Although numerically the first of the class, D9001 *St. Paddy* was actually first to enter service, five days before D9000, on 23 February 1961.

Nos 55009 *Alycidon* and 55019 *Royal Highland Fusilier* are seen at New Bridge near Pickering on 26 April 1985. No. 55009 had just had a power unit changed, another first in Deltic preservation; power unit No. 419, having suffered flashover damage to its generator, was replaced by one of the spares purchased by the DPS, No. 424, which was last fitted to No. 55017. The steam crane at New Bridge was used for this. On the following day test runs were carried out using both Deltics, with one coach sandwiched in the middle.

It is 23 August 1985 and No. 55019 *Royal Highland Fusilier* and No. 9000 *Royal Scots Grey* look superb together as they are reunited at their spiritual home of Haymarket depot, Edinburgh, for an open day. By now, No. 9000 has had her route indicator restored to working order. A photograph that sums up for me the pride and care taken by the preserved locomotives' new custodians.

No. 9000 *Royal Scots Grey* again at Haymarket, in company of one of the Scottish Region's stalwart Class 27s. They did sterling service in pairs, top-and-tailing the Edinburgh–Glasgow shuttles, before the Class 47/7s took over. I can still hear the reverberating Sulzer engines as they blasted through the rather smelly tunnel out of Queen Street station and got to grips with Cowlairs incline.

The Deltics' remarkable preservation story continues with this shot of No. 55015 *Tulyar* at Hampton Loade while visiting on the Severn Valley Railway in 1987. She is in charge of a mixed rake, including some of the railway's beautifully restored LNER Gresley teak stock. The SVR prides itself in its pre-nationalisation coaching stock.

Kidderminster station on the Severn Valley Railway in May 1987 sees No. 55015 *Tulyar* again. Behind the locomotive is the BR line to Birmingham. Notice the headboard in the style of a Deltic nameplate. She had become the DPS's third locomotive the previous year following purchase from the private owner, who had saved her from scrap.

Both surviving racehorses reunited at Grosmont as No. 55009 *Alycidon* shares the headshunt with sister No. 55015 *Tulyar*, c. 1989. Eventually, the remote location of the NYMR for many of the DPS volunteers, together with the need for a permanent covered facility, were factors in the decision to establish the society's excellent purpose-built shed at Barrow Hill.

We now fast forward to Rawtenstall in 1996 and my first experience of one of the excellent diesel galas at the East Lancashire Railway. The DPS's D9019 *Royal Highland Fusilier* looks almost totally authentic for the 1960s, apart from the ETH connections and blanked cab quarter-light windows. She has also had her rooftop horns restored, being one of only three Deltics to carry them, along with D9020 and D9021.

Also at Rawtenstall in 1996, the NRM's Deltic No. 55002 *The King's Own Yorkshire Light Infantry* gleams in the evening sun in this telephoto shot. The ELR diesel galas have been a regular event for us in recent years, and we look forward to the time when unique survivor, Metro-Vick Co-Bo D5705, is the star of the show.

30 November 1996 at Edinburgh Waverley: the momentous occasion is the imminent departure of 'The Deltic Deliverance' railtour, the first Deltic-hauled passenger train on the main line since 2 January 1982. Appropriately, it was D9000 *Royal Scots Grey* that had this honour, just as she brought the curtain down almost fifteen years previously. Sadly, this maiden run was cut short at Berwick after only 57 miles because of a minor fire in an exhaust collector drum.

The Midland Railway Centre at Butterley in Derbyshire was the first preservation home to No. 55015 *Tulyar*, where she is seen on a short train of maroon Mk1s in 1997. The MRC has neither the length nor the gradients of the North Yorkshire Moors Railway, so a Deltic-hauled trip there is, by comparison, pedestrian to say the least. *Tulyar* is now in the final stages of a long-awaited return to the main line after a major overhaul at Barrow Hill.

It is now 7 June 2003 and the 1990s are long gone. A Deltic Preservation Society railtour is to take us to King's Cross, originating at our old stamping ground of Newcastle with No. 55019 *Royal Highland Fusilier*, once again sporting blue livery with yellow plated-over headcode panels. The route took us via Lincoln in both directions, giving us 566 miles of Deltic haulage.

Having arrived at King's Cross from Newcastle behind No. 55019, we were pleasantly surprised to find No. 9016 *Gordon Highlander* in her controversial Porterbrook livery backing on to the empty stock. I didn't object to the purple colour scheme and black nameplates as much as the Ford Cortina light clusters!

Back at the East Lancashire Railway in July 2009 we see No. 55022 *Royal Scots Grey* at Heywood, during another one of their galas. In order to reach Heywood, trains leaving Bury Bolton Street have to climb steeply as they negotiate a sharp curve and what can only be described as a hump-backed bridge in order to cross the Metrolink. This is always an exciting, noisy departure.

No. 55022 *Royal Scots Grey* again passing Bootham near York on a GBRf staff charter from Scarborough on 24 July 2010. The locomotive's owner Martin Walker can be seen passing instructions from the front coach window to the crew member hanging out of the rear cab! The rake of stock includes BR MkI and MkII and a vintage Pullman car.

On 4 December 2010 No. 55022 *Royal Scots Grey* is captured entering a snowy Newcastle Central from the King Edward VII Bridge with Spitfire Railtours' 'Edinburgh Explorer'. This had originated in Preston and came to Newcastle via Wigan, Bolton and Leeds. I believe this was one of many trips marketed as Christmas shopping specials, but there would have been a sizeable number of 'bashers' on board too!

A truly unexpected turn of events is depicted here on 12 April 2011, with No. 55022 *Royal Scots Grey* closer to the east coast than she ever got on the main line of that name. She was on hire to GB Railfreight and was employed on mineral trains from North Blyth to the Alcan aluminium smelter at Lynemouth. Note the radio aerial on her nose.

Two generations of east-coast power are on show here at North Blyth, with No. 55022 contrasting with an offshore wind turbine. Once home to a fleet of hardworking J27s, North Blyth shed was located nearby, providing motive power for coal trains to feed the power station here, now long gone. On the other side of the River Blyth today is NAREC, a research centre dedicated to the development of renewable energy.

A general view of the terminal at North Blyth with No. 55022, showing the distinctive silos into which incoming ships would discharge their cargo of aluminium ore. So here we are, thirty years since the Deltics were in revenue-earning service on BR, and No. 9000 is still doing a useful job at the age of fifty.

Running light engine towards the Blyth and Tyne main line No. 55022 *Royal Scots Grey* puts on a show for the massed photographers on the A189 'Spine Road' bridge between Cambois and Sleekburn. She is laying a smokescreen that is about to obliterate No. 66105, which is waiting for the single-line token.

Looking west from the same vantage point on another day in April 2011 and this time No. 55022 is hauling a train of empties from Lynemouth. Sadly, Northumberland lost a major employer less than a year later when the smelter closed. Lynemouth power station continues to contribute to the National Grid and generates coal traffic as well as electricity.

The idyllic setting of Darnholm on the 1 in 49 climb from Grosmont to Goathland is the location for this shot of No. 55002 *The King's Own Yorkshire Light Infantry*, taken on 17 September 2011. She has, at last, lost the two-tone green livery she had worn since 1980, carried longer than any 'authentic' colour scheme. The stock includes an ex-GWR observation saloon and a 1920s Pullman car.

A night shot of No. 55022 *Royal Scots Grey* on Pathfinder's 'York Flyer' railtour at Coventry, on 2 June 2012. This tour originated at Didcot and ran via Manchester Victoria to York. The return journey was on the East Coast Main Line, then through North London before being diverted via Coventry, where she had to run around the stock, eventually arriving in Didcot three hours late!

On 1 July 2012 I paid my first visit to Barrow Hill and was able to see for myself the impressive facility in which the Deltic Preservation Society is able to maintain and restore its fleet. New members are always welcome, as are willing volunteers. On this occasion, the NRM's No. 55002 *The King's Own Yorkshire Light Infantry* is undergoing maintenance.

D9015 *Tulyar* is well on the way to restoration in the DPS shed at Barrow Hill on 1 July 2012. There is still work to be done by the team of dedicated volunteers, but it won't be too long before she is once again hauling trains. I for one am looking forward to this, as I have not travelled on No. 55015 since December 1981, the only one I have missed in preservation.

Also inside the Deltic Preservation Society building at Barrow Hill on the same day was the cab of No. 55021 *Argyll & Sutherland Highlander*, perched on a Lowmac wagon. The cab of No. 55008 *The Green Howards*, complete with train simulator, was outside on a road trailer. I suppose a Deltic cab is better than no Deltic at all, but I find this a little macabre, like a severed head on display.

Six days after Barrow Hill, and I am once again at an East Lancashire Railway diesel gala. At Heywood on 7 July 2012, No. 55002 *The King's Own Yorkshire Light Infantry* is running around her train. These events have provided some amazing spectacles, including nine Class 14s on one train and, best of all, five Deltics providing 14,850 hp up front, an event I sadly missed.

A close-up of that Gateshead style of Deltic nameplate on No. 55002, with narrower font and rounded corners. One authentic Gateshead touch that is lacking is a thick layer of black muck, although she is doing her best, judging by the oil running down from the exhaust port.

By poking my camera inside an open engine-room window, I was able to take this photograph of one of the Napier Deltic power units of No. 55002. The Deltic engine is an incredible piece of engineering, which found a number of disparate applications, including naval vessels and even as a pump on a New York City fire tender!

Looking splendid in the run-around loop at Rawtenstall is No. 55002 *The King's Own Yorkshire Light Infantry*. I have a soft spot for No. 55002, as the sole surviving Gateshead Deltic. As D9002, she was the first Deltic to be out-shopped in the new BR 'monastral' blue livery in October 1966.

Bury Bolton Street on 8 July 2012: I was at last about to experience travel behind double-headed Deltics. D9016 *Gordon Highlander* is being coupled to No. 55002 *The King's Own Yorkshire Light Infantry*. Note the difference in bogie construction, No. 55002 is riding on the later cast version while D9016's are fabricated.

View from the train window between Rawtenstall and Ramsbottom as our double-header of D9016 and No. 55002 heads south. Anyone who has ever experienced Deltic haulage either on the main line or a preserved railway will be able to imagine the assault on the senses that is taking place here with that noise, that smoke and that smell from the Napier engines.

A solo study of D9016 *Gordon Highlander* at Ramsbottom station on the East Lancashire Railway. During the brilliant diesel galas, this is where hordes of enthusiasts race across the footbridge as two trains cross here. A close look at D9016 revealed much corrosion due to years of outdoor storage. Happily, she is now receiving some long-awaited bodywork attention.

Passing the place of Ian's employment for the past twenty-seven years – Heaton traincare depot east of Newcastle – is D9009 *Alycidon* with 'The Elizabethan' railtour on 25 July 2012. This was a duty she shared with another heritage railway miracle, new-build Peppercorn A1 No. 60163 *Tornado*. Ian joined the railway as an apprentice fitter in 1983 and he is currently employed as a production team leader at Heaton.

Another year, another East Lancashire Railway diesel gala – and on 6 July 2013 No. 55022 *Royal Scots Grey* makes an interesting comparison with the Class 40 Preservation Society's D335 and Bury Valiant Group's No. 50015 *Valiant* at Castlecroft, Bury. Three products of English Electric's famous Vulcan Foundry on display, totalling 8,000 horsepower.

D9009 *Alycidon* gleams in the morning sun as she arrives with empty stock at Bury on 7 July 2013. Bury Bolton Street station had been the terminus of the unique 1200v DC third-rail electric service from Manchester Victoria, which closed in 1991 to be replaced by the Metrolink system. Just off to the right of this photograph is the Trackside bar with a wonderful selection of real beer.

The Deltic Preservation Society's D9009 looks fantastic as she waits at Ramsbottom station on the same day. By this time D9009 had been in preservation for thirty-one years and looks as good as new, thanks to the hard work of the DPS volunteers at Barrow Hill. This colour scheme of two-tone green with small yellow panels is, in my humble opinion, the most attractive Deltic livery.

On 14 September 2013 D9009 *Alycidon* is back on the North Yorkshire Moors Railway once more. Here she is working hard up the 1 in 49 gradient from Grosmont to Goathland. On this stretch, the route crosses the Eller Beck several times, giving passengers glimpses of waterfalls and steep gorges. In 2010 Bridge no. 30 was replaced at a cost of £750,000.

Pathfinder Tours' 'Winter Settler' railtour on 28 December 2013 began at Crewe hauled by a Class 67. At Derby, D9009 *Alycidon* took over for the spectacular trip over the Settle & Carlisle line to the border city. She returned via the Tyne Valley and the East Coast Main Line where she is seen at York.

12 April 2014 marked the welcome return of No. 55002 *The King's Own Yorkshire Light Infantry* to the main line with 'The Deltic Aberdonian' railtour from York to Aberdeen and back. This was organised by 52A Railtours (named after the old Gateshead BR shed code). Here No. 55002 takes a breather at Edinburgh Waverley, having recorded a magical 100 mph on the way here.

No. 55002 has now arrived at Aberdeen with 'The Deltic Aberdonian'. We had treated ourselves to posh tickets in the front coach with cooked breakfast served to us, as we crossed the Forth Bridge heading north. Once in the Granite City we sampled a few malts in a wonderful old whisky bar before returning to the station for the return trip.

Leaving Dundee behind her, No. 55002 is seen making her way onto the Tay Bridge with 'The Deltic Aberdonian'. To the left can be seen the remains of Bouch's original bridge, which was famously swept away in a storm in 1879, along with a North British Railway 4-4-0, her train and all who were aboard.

The Forth Bridge, opened in 1890, never fails to impress, and is best seen from the water's edge. It is a stupendous piece of British Victorian engineering, perhaps over-engineered in reaction to what had happened on the Tay. No. 55002 is threading through the girders with 'The Deltic Aberdonian' as she returns south.

13 September 2014 at Grosmont, NYMR, sees No. 55002 *The King's Own Yorkshire Light Infantry* with another National Railway Museum artefact, pioneer Class 37 D6700, both being prepared for the day's services. The 309-strong Class 37 was another English Electric success story, and many are still in service on the main line today, fifty-five years after D6700 took to the rails.

No. 55002 pauses at Goathland on 13 September 2014. This charming location has served as Aidensfield on ITV's *Heartbeat* and the station became Hogsmeade in the *Harry Potter* series of films, with a direct service from platform 9¾ at King's Cross hauled by a GWR 'Hall', of all things!

The seat of power, inside the cab of No. 55002 at the NYMR. Because of the size of the nose ends, the driver's position was very high. Much soundproofing was necessary in the bulkheads between cabs and engine room, and a rubber curtain was introduced to try and deaden the noise further. Notice the mix of original instruments and modern communication equipment for main-line use.

We come to 2015 and, on 4 July, D9009 *Alycidon* was used on a Pathfinder railtour from Derby to Kingswear. Here she is in the early morning at Derby Midland before departure. The route would include such delights as the Lickey incline and the Devon sea walls, both uncharted territory for me in terms of Deltic haulage.

Several hours later we headed across the River Dart from Kingswear to Dartmouth to sample the local beer, and I was able to capture this shot of D9009 through a forest of masts in very unfamiliar surroundings. South of Paignton, the line is now in the hands of the Torbay & Dartmouth Steam Railway.

The GWR train shed at Kingswear looks a little incongruous with former East Coast thoroughbred D9009 in attendance. Here she is ticking over, awaiting the return journey to Derby. The Deltic worked the train as far as Landor Street Junction in Birmingham for operational reasons, and No. 66089 took us the rest of the way back to Derby.